MILA BOUTAN

text and drawings

Picasso and the Great Painters

 Thames & Hudson

Picasso

Have you heard of Picasso? Perhaps you know all about him.

He's the artist who once said:

'If I don't have any blue, I use red instead.'

He's famous for painting people with their faces pointing

in different directions, or with their noses the wrong way round.

You might think that he didn't know how to draw.

But that's where you'd be wrong. When Picasso was just six years old,

his father gave him some brushes and pencils and told him:

'You paint better than the great Italian artist **Raphael**.'

Pablo Picasso
was born in **Spain** in **1881**,
into a family of artists.
He was taught to **paint** by his **father**,
who showed him the work of the
great painters of the past:
first, Spanish artists such as **El Greco**,
Zurbarán, **Velázquez** and **Goya**,
followed by French artists such as
Chardin, **Delacroix** and **Manet**, and
then painters from his own time, such as
Cézanne, **Van Gogh** and **Matisse**.

Picasso didn't copy these other
artists. He was inspired by them,
and tried to understand their paintings
by reworking, changing and twisting
them. You'll find some of their
works in this book, and you might
even learn to see them
the way Picasso did.

Picasso and Velázquez

Diego Velázquez was born in Seville in 1599.
After years of training, **Velázquez** went to Madrid, the capital of Spain,
where he became the favourite painter of King Philip IV.

His most famous painting is called **Las Meninas**, which means
The Ladies-in-Waiting. It's a portrait of Princess **Margarita**,
the king's daughter, with her playmates. This extraordinary picture
still amazes both the public and other artists.

Picasso was fascinated by this painting
and knew every inch of it by heart.
He knew the **colours** and the **composition**,
but he kept on looking,
trying to get inside the picture,
to **take it to pieces** and
see how it was made.

So this is what he did:

he shut himself in a room with his blank **canvases**,

his **brushes** and his **paints**,

and day after day, night after night,

he thought about the painting and everything in it.

Margarita,

the **princess** who shines like the **sun** in the middle of the painting!

The **Meninas** themselves,
who bow towards her respectfully.

The Meninas
are the princess's
ladies-in-waiting.

The **boy** with his
leg stretched out
and his foot on the
dog's back.

The **rectangle of light**
made by a man who is opening or closing the door.
He lets **light** into the room and gives
a sense of **perspective**.

The **windows** that light the right side of the picture.

Picasso wanted to **understand**
everything that Velázquez was trying to do.

Look at how **Velázquez** composed his picture,
and where he positioned his figures.

They are not **standing in a straight line**, like in a **photograph**.
Instead, they stand like actors on a stage or pieces on a chessboard.
They are broad at the base and narrow at the top, like little **pyramids**
in a wide open space, under a very high ceiling.

This **ribbon-like** line shows the sense of **depth** and **volume**.

What about the artist?

He's taller than all the other figures.

He holds a palette and a brush,
and his canvas forms a **diagonal** line.

But **who** is the artist painting?
What do you think? It can't
be the little princess, because
he can only see her back!
Look closely. Get out
your magnifying glass,
like a detective!

Have you noticed
the **mirror**?

**What can you see
in the mirror?**

Picasso painted his own Meninas.

Look closely and see how he did it.

Picasso asked himself lots of questions.
What might happen if I **cover** the windows? Or if I **light**
the **lamps** on the ceiling? Or if I **close** the door at the back?
What if I make **Margarita** wear a **yellow dress**?
What if I make her **square**? What if I make her **taller** or **shorter**?
It would change everything – the **perspective**, the **shadows**,
the **light**, the **colours**.

Look at the **shades** of **grey** and **white** he used in this painting.
How is the **left side** of the room different from the **right side**?
On the left, the **tall artist** stands behind his canvas,
and the **kneeling maid** wears a very detailed **dress**.
On the right are **blank white shapes**.

This version is mostly **red** and **black** – it looks like **night** has fallen!
Where have the **windows** gone? The lamps on the ceiling are **lit**.
Can you see the two figures with big hands on the top right?
Picasso also included them in the other paintings
but they are not as easy to see.

This painting is filled with **triangles** that **fit together**. What are they for? Do they create a stronger sense of **volume** and an impression of **depth**? Or are they just there to highlight some of the details?

Now look below. See if you can find the **artist**. What **shape** is he? And what about the boy's **leg**? Can you see the head of the **dwarf**? Where is the **man** in the doorway? Which parts of the painting are **bright** and which are in **shadow**? Where is the **light** falling?

What about the dog?

Picasso makes you stop and think about the lines and spaces, and the relationships between colours and shapes.

Picasso and swords

Picasso
was Spanish,
and loved **bullfighting**.
Throughout his life he drew
bulls. In **Spain**, bullfights are
festivals and Picasso loved the sense
of **celebration** and **sunshine**, **light** and
shade, the noise and the crowds. During
the final years of his life, he often chose to
paint figures holding matadors' **swords**.
Like them, Picasso imagined he was loved
by the cheering crowd.

He also spent a lot of time studying the
work of another artist who loved Spain:
Édouard Manet.

Could this painting of a matador
by Manet have been a starting
point for Picasso?

Manet
A Matador

What do you think of this portrait of a **man with a sword**? He's sitting on the ground, with his **legs** sticking out and his **hair** untidy, and he's holding a **flower** in his **hand**. Does his face look **frightened**? Is he about to **fight** a **bull** with his thin **sword**? Is the flower a **gift** for his **lady love**? Is he a **dwarf**?

Velázquez
The Dwarf Sebastián de Morra

He looks like this dwarf painted by **Velázquez**, without a hat, but with the same **green** tunic and **red** cloak with **gold** braid.

15

This man has a hat and a ponytail like a **bullfighter**.
Picasso called him The Matador — the name for the bullfighter
who **kills** the **bull**. He's smoking a cigar and seems quite relaxed.
Do you think the bullfight's over and the **bull** is **dead**?

Do you think he looks like the **matador** painted
by Manet, which Picasso admired?
Turn back a page and compare the two.
What differences can you spot?

Here's a **soldier**, dressed all in **red**
and wearing a large **hat** with a **feather**.
The background is **red** and **gold**
like the **Spanish flag**.

Picasso and Manet

Édouard Manet
was born in **Paris** in 1832. He wasn't a good pupil, but he had a gift for painting, and became one of the most famous young artists of the day.

In 1863, his painting **Le Déjeuner sur l'herbe (Lunch on the Grass)** caused a **scandal**, because it was so different from the paintings that the public expected to see. People didn't understand what it was about. They thought it looked like **Manet** hadn't finished it and they didn't like the colours.

Picasso loved this **unusual** painting. In an attempt to solve its mysteries, he produced a **series** of 27 paintings and hundreds of drawings, changing the figures and their surroundings.

Manet
The Piper

This is **Le Déjeuner sur l'herbe**.

On the grass are two **fully dressed** men, speaking to a
nude woman, while another woman has her feet in the water.
Under the trees there's a blue tablecloth, with a **picnic** on it.

But does this painting actually tell a story?
Perhaps it's more about **colour** and **light** and **shade**.
Look how the **white** contrasts with the **black**.
The shadowy forest and the two men in their frock coats
create a **dark frame** while the **light**, focused on the bodies
of the two women, gives a sense of **depth**.

My goodness!

What has **Picasso** done here?
The picnic and the **blue tablecloth**
have vanished. The talking man
and the nude woman fill
the whole space.

The bending woman is
standing in a **square blue pond**,
which looks like a tablecloth.

Now everything
has turned **green**.
The **forest** has
closed in around
the figures.
The **light** is
focused on
the woman in
the water.

20

Here, everyone is **naked**. The **man**, perhaps the artist, has become wider and longer. The blue pond fills all the space in the **centre** of the picture.

The woman with her feet in the water is still there. Another **nude man**, lying on the grass, forms another area of white.

In almost all the pictures in this series, the sitting man's **hand** looks very large and is **outstretched** to show that he's speaking.

Now look at the **walking stick** in his other hand. It's facing in a different **direction**. Does this change the **balance** of the picture?

The woman has a rounded figure. She seems to be daydreaming or listening, her arms draped around her body.

What about the forest?

Now the figures are by the coast, and there's a **boat** out on the water. The picnic has reappeared, but the tablecloth is now white. The picture looks full of **sunshine.**

What about the man's beret?

Sometimes it's there, sometimes it's not.

The man is now **bald** and has **no beard.** In fact, **he looks like Picasso** himself, and the woman looks like **Jacqueline**, his model and companion.

By showing us what can be done with this **mysterious** painting, **Picasso** allows us to understand both his own work and **Manet**'s picture, a hundred years after it was first painted.

Picasso and still-life painting

Here is a still-life painting by Picasso.

What is a **still life**?

It's a **painting** in which the **artist** depicts everyday **objects**.

There's no story – the objects are shown just as they are.

Picasso painted a lot of still lifes. In these pictures, he doesn't try to **imitate** what he sees. Instead, he **expresses** what he **feels** and tries to make people **understand**.

In the picture opposite, you can see two **pears** and two **apples** on a **red** table, in front of a **grey** wall.

It all looks very simple.

But in fact it's not simple at all.

Look at the **fruit:** it's the **colours** that create the shapes. The strong light coming from the right makes the **pears** look longer. Their shapes are **pointed**, like the red **table.** They form two yellow **triangles** on top of a big red **triangle.** Now look at the two **round apples.** They contrast with the triangles and make them stand out. The shadows contain another round shape.

Picasso did not invent still-life painting, of course.

He learned from the work of the painters of the past.

Francisco de Zurbarán, born in 1598 in **Spain**,
was another painter that **Picasso** learned from.

See how simple
his **compositions** are.

Just some jugs, some apples, some quinces, a basket.
But he uses them to make **amazing** still lifes.

Jean-Baptiste-Siméon Chardin, born in Paris in 1699,
was one of the **greatest French painters of the 18th century**.
Here is a still life he painted: a **burnt orange** bowl, a **silver** goblet,
three **apples** and two **chestnuts** on a **green** background.
It looks very simple, don't you think? But it's far from it!

What **Chardin** shows us is the **reflection** of the red and white **apples**
on the **goblet** and the **bowl**. We can't see inside the bowl,
but the **spoon** gives us the sense that it is **hollow**.

This is a self-portrait by Chardin.

He wears a scarf tied over his ears – was it a cold day?
He probably painted in the kitchen because it was warmer there.
On the table stood a silver goblet and some fruit. He didn't always
paint the same things, but the sun outside the window could make
objects look different. If a cloud passed over, the light would change.
So would he rub out his painting and start again?
No, he'd just start a brand new canvas.

27

Paul Cézanne was born in 1839 in
Aix-en-Provence, France. **Picasso** said of him:

'He was my one and only master.
You may think that I looked at his pictures.
In fact, I spent years studying them.'

What does **Cézanne** show us in the painting below?
An apple, a pear and two small plums.
What is important is not the drawing but the **colour harmonies**
– the tiny **brushstrokes** of green, yellow and red blended together
that make up the fruits. Are they coloured lumps or more than that?
Cézanne leaves it up to you to decide.

This still life by **Picasso** is more unusual than the first one.
First of all, look at the unusual way that the objects are arranged.
Compare them with the painting on the previous page!
Instead of forming a **horizontal row**, like in a shop window, they have been
placed **behind one another**. So that we can see all of them,
Picasso has **piled them up vertically**.

The **light** is red almost everywhere, and some **shadows** fall to
the **right** and some to the **left**, which looks rather strange!
However, we can still understand what **Picasso** wanted to show:
these round, hollow objects reflect the light. **Picasso** **lets us see**
that you can paint a still life without following the rules.

Picasso and Van Gogh

Picasso loved artists who had **new** and **original** ideas.
Vincent Van Gogh was a **Dutch painter**, born in 1853,
barely **thirty years before Picasso**. It was in **France**
that he painted some of his most **extraordinary** pictures.

Van Gogh lived only for **painting**. His only **friend** was his **brother Theo**. In his **letters** to Theo, **Vincent** talked about his paintings and everything that he wanted them to say. **Vincent** is the name he signed on his paintings. He used **raw paints**, without mixing the colours, and painted in **red** and **green**, **blue** and **yellow**. He used his **paintbrush** like a **sculptor**, in **broad strokes** to show **movement**.

Vincent once said:
'I make sculptures with paint.'

And here's what **Picasso** said about him:
'It's amazing to invent new subjects, like potatoes or old shoes. That's really something!'

Now discover how **Picasso** created a portrait based on **Van Gogh**'s work…

Look at this self-portrait by **Van Gogh** and see how the brushstrokes change direction. They are **vertical** around the edges of the **hat**, they spread out from the **eyes** across the **forehead**, **cheeks** and **beard**, and they curve over the **shoulders** to form the **jacket**. The **eyes**, surrounded by **red** and **green** (**complementary colours**), gaze out at us with great **intensity**.

Now here is a painting by **Picasso**, inspired by **Van Gogh**'s self-portrait. It's easy to see the **thick, clear strokes** that he has used to paint the **beard**, the **hat**, the **lips** and the **tongue**. He has also added an **ice cream cone** for fun – Picasso liked to include touches of **humour** in his paintings, as you might have noticed!

Picasso and El Greco

El Greco was a great painter who was born in Greece in 1541 but lived in Spain. His name means 'The Greek' in Spanish.

He mostly painted **religious** subjects but didn't try to make them **realistic**. His figures often have distorted, strangely shaped bodies, with **long legs** and **tiny heads**, and arms stretching up to the sky. They look as if they're **floating in space**.

The **colours** and the **light** are startling too: bright **yellows**, **greens** and **pinks**.

He was very different from the other painters of his day!

He didn't paint what he saw, but what he wanted to make people feel. **Picasso** did the same thing.

El Greco was almost forgotten for 250 years, but he was rediscovered at the same time that **Picasso** was studying. **El Greco**'s work went on to inspire many young artists.

Picasso
Boy Leading a Horse

35

It is easy to recognize a portrait by **El Greco**: the **figures** are tall and dressed in **black**, the **faces** are **long** and elegant and the **background** is **black** too.

You can also tell by the **stylized** hands.

In **Picasso**'s version, everything **stays in place**: the palette, the big white ruff and the paintbrush.

Look at the **hand** that's holding the **paintbrush**. See how **delicate** and **graceful** it is.

Who is this?

This is the poet **Jaime Sabartés**, who was **Picasso**'s secretary. He is wearing a **ruff** and a hat like a Spanish **gentleman** from the days of **El Greco**. But his **glasses** look quite **modern**.

Look again!

Look at this portrait of Cardinal Guevara in his spectacles, also by **El Greco**. Do you think **Picasso** knew about it? He painted his secretary in the style of an **El Greco** painting. He must have been very fond of **Sabartés**.

Picasso and Cranach

Lucas Cranach the Younger was a great **German** painter of the **Renaissance**, born in 1515. He **invented** a new style of painting men and women. **Picasso** loved the work of Cranach and other painters who were original, **just like he was**.

Cranach's father was also a painter, and is known as **Lucas Cranach the Elder**. He painted the **young woman** on the right. Both ladies look like models from a fashion magazine. Look at their **hats**, **necklaces** and **rings**.

Here is a painting by **Picasso**, showing a **rich lady** dressed in beautiful **jewelry**. How is she like **Cranach**'s lady? How is she different?

Choose a painting that you like and look at it closely. Some paintings make you happy just to look at them. You can almost hear the birds sing, feel the warm sun, and smell the flowers. Paintings can make you feel all kinds of things, but they all have something to say. Do what Picasso did, and try to express what you feel in your drawings, without copying other people's work.

What are you waiting for? Pick up a pencil and draw!

Paint

Margarita

FIRST, PHOTOCOPY THESE TWO PAGES. THEN CUT OUT THE SHAPES AND ARRANGE THEM IN THE ROOM ON PAGE 43.

Inside these shapes, draw your own versions of the people from the painting: the princess, her maids, and the dog. Include yourself as the artist, with your brushes or pencils!

You could draw some speech bubbles and add what they are saying to each other.

the man

the princess

the painting

the artist

Or are they staying quiet?

Are they all ready to take their places in the picture?

the kneeling maid

the dwarf

The standing maid looks rather cross.

the boy

the dog

the mirror

2 figures

the standing maid

What is she saying to the princess?

NOW USE YOUR OWN PENCILS, PAINTBRUSHES AND SCISSORS
TO MAKE YOUR OWN PAINTING.

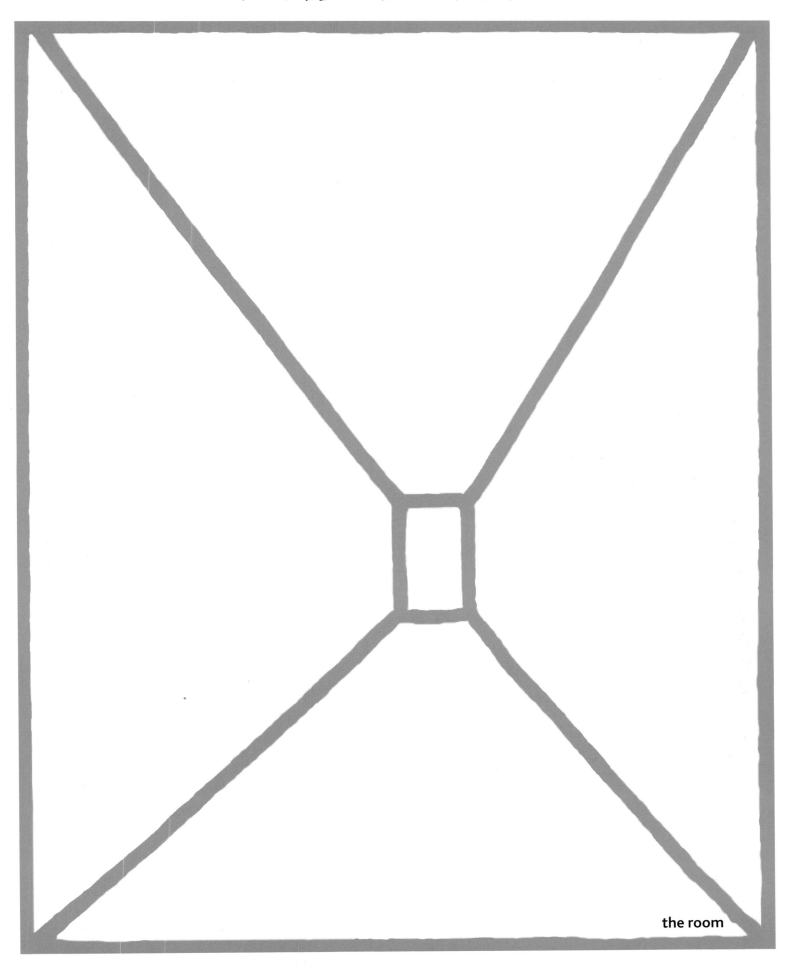

the room

PAINT YOUR OWN STILL LIFE

Now you've come to the end of this book, look back through the pages.
Which paintings caught your attention? Which ones did you like best?

PAINTINGS IN THIS BOOK

Pablo Picasso
*Self-Portrait
with a Palette*
Paris, summer—
autumn 1906
Philadelphia
Museum of Art

Pablo Picasso
Child with a Dove
1901
Private collection,
London

Diego Velázquez
Las Meninas
1657
Museo del Prado,
Madrid

Pablo Picasso
Princess Margarita
Cannes,
14 September 1957
Museu Picasso,
Barcelona

Pablo Picasso
Las Meninas
(after Velázquez)
Cannes,
17 August 1957
Museu Picasso,
Barcelona

Pablo Picasso
Las Meninas
Cannes,
19 September 1957
Museu Picasso,
Barcelona

Pablo Picasso
Las Meninas
18 September 1957
Museu Picasso,
Barcelona

Pablo Picasso
Las Meninas
Cannes,
3 October 1957
Museu Picasso,
Barcelona

Pablo Picasso
*Seated Man with
Sword and Flower*
Mougins,
2 August—
27 September 1969
Adela Vilato Collection

Diego Velázquez
*The Dwarf Sebastián
de Morra*
1644
Museo del Prado,
Madrid

Édouard Manet
A Matador
1866–67
The Metropolitan
Museum of Art,
New York

Pablo Picasso
The Matador
4 October 1970
Musée Picasso, Paris

Pablo Picasso
*Seated Musketeer
with Sword*
Mougins,
19 July 1969
Maya Ruiz Collection

Édouard Manet
The Piper
1866
Musée d'Orsay, Paris

Édouard Manet
*Le Déjeuner sur l'herbe
(Lunch on the Grass)*
1863
Musée d'Orsay, Paris

Pablo Picasso
*Le Déjeuner
sur l'herbe*
(after Manet)
Mougins,
10 August 1961
Private collection

Pablo Picasso
Le Déjeuner sur l'herbe
(after Manet)
Mougins,
17 June 1962
Musée Picasso, Paris

Pablo Picasso
Le Déjeuner sur l'herbe
(after Manet)
Mougins,
13 July 1961
Musée Picasso, Paris

Pablo Picasso
Le Déjeuner sur l'herbe
(after Manet)
Vauvenargues,
4 March and
30 July 1960
Helly Nahmad Collection

Pablo Picasso
Le Déjeuner sur l'herbe
(after Manet)
Mougins,
30 July 1961
Louisiana Museum
of Modern Art,
Humlebaek, Denmark

Pablo Picasso
Pears and Apples
Paris, autumn 1908
James W. Alsdorf
Collection, Chicago

Francisco de Zurbarán
*Still Life with Lemons,
Oranges and a Rose,* 1663
Norton Simon Museum,
Pasadena

Francisco de Zurbarán
Still Life
c. 1660
Museu Nacional d'Art
de Catalunya,
Barcelona

Francisco de Zurbarán
*Still Life
with Quinces*
Museu Nacional d'Art
de Catalunya, Barcelona

Jean-Baptiste-
Siméon Chardin
*Self-Portrait with
an Eyeshade*
1775
Musée du Louvre, Paris

Jean-Baptiste-
Siméon Chardin
The Silver Goblet
c. 1768
Musée du Louvre, Paris

Paul Cézanne
*Self-Portrait
with Palette*
1884
Stiftung Sammlung
Bührle, Zurich

Paul Cézanne
*Still Life: Pear and
Green Apples, c.* 1873
Musée de l'Orangerie,
Paris

Pablo Picasso
Pitcher and Bowls
spring–summer 1908
The State Hermitage
Museum, St Petersburg

Vincent Van Gogh
Sunflowers
Arles,
late August 1888
National Gallery,
London

Vincent Van Gogh
Van Gogh's Chair
20 November 1888
National Gallery,
London

Pablo Picasso
*Bust of a Woman
with Striped Hat*
3 June 1939
Musée Picasso, Paris

Vincent Van Gogh
*Self-Portrait with
Felt Hat*
1888
Van Gogh Museum,
Amsterdam

Pablo Picasso
*Man with Straw Hat
and Ice Cream Cone*
Mougins,
30 August 1938
Musée Picasso, Paris

El Greco
*St Martin and
the Beggar*
1597–99
National Gallery of Art,
Washington DC

El Greco
The Annunciation
1596–1600
Museo del Prado,
Madrid

Pablo Picasso
Boy Leading a Horse
Paris, 1905–6
Museum of Modern Art,
New York

El Greco
*An Artist (Probably Jorge
Manuel Theotokopoulos)*
c. 1600–5
Museo de Bellas Artes,
Seville

Pablo Picasso
Portrait of an Artist
(after El Greco)
22 February 1950
Private collection,
Lucerne

Pablo Picasso
Portrait of Jaime Sabartés
Royan,
22 October 1939
Museu Picasso,
Barcelona

El Greco
*Portrait of a Cardinal,
Probably Cardinal Don
Fernando Niño de Guevara*
c. 1600
The Metropolitan
Museum of Art, New York

Lucas Cranach
the Younger
Portrait of a Woman
1564
Kunsthistorisches
Museum, Vienna

Pablo Picasso
Portrait of a Young Girl,
(after Cranach
the Younger)
Cannes, 4 July 1958
Musée Picasso, Paris

Lucas Cranach the Elder
David and Bathsheba
1526
Gemäldegalerie, Berlin